First published in Great Britain in 2015 by Canongate Books Ltd,
14 High Street, Edinburgh EH1 1TE

www.canongate.tv

1

British Library Cataloguing-in-Publication Data
A catalogue record for this book is available on
request from the British Library

ISBN 978 1 78211 641 7

PEANUTS written and drawn by Charles M. Schulz
Edited by Jenny Lord and Andy Miller
Art Direction: Rafaela Romaya
Design: Chris Gale
Layout: Stuart Polson

Printed in Latvia by Livonia Print, SIA

THE BUMPER BOOK OF PEANUTS®

Schulz

CANONGATE
Edinburgh · London

AAAUGGH!

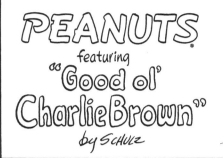

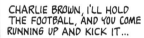

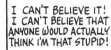

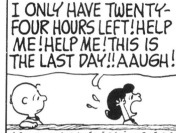

BASEBALL

PEANUTS

MY HEART IS FULL ON THE DAY I FIRST GO OUT TO THE OL' BALL FIELD...

I LOVE THE SMELL OF THE HORSEHIDE, THE GRASSY OUTFIELD AND THE DUSTY INFIELD...I LOVE THE MEMORIES..THE HOPES...AND THE DREAMS FOR THE NEW SEASON..

AH! THERE IT IS! MY PITCHER'S MOUND...COVERED WITH TRADITION..

AND DANDELIONS!

PEANUTS

THIS PITCHER'S MOUND IS COVERED WITH DANDELIONS

DON'T TOUCH THEM, CHARLIE BROWN!

DON'T YOU DARE HURT ALL THOSE INNOCENT DANDELIONS! THEY'RE BEAUTIFUL! DON'T YOU DARE CUT THEM DOWN!

BESIDES, YOU MAY NOT KNOW IT, BUT YOU LOOK KIND OF CUTE STANDING THERE SURROUNDED BY DANDELIONS..

I DON'T WANT TO LOOK CUTE!!

PEANUTS

HERE WE GO... THE FIRST PITCH OF THE SEASON..

POW!

IT'S KIND OF PEACEFUL LYING HERE AMONG THE DANDELIONS..

PEANUTS

IT'S GETTING DARK..I GUESS THAT'S ENOUGH PRACTICE FOR TODAY..

YOU THINK I DON'T CARE ABOUT OUR TEAM, DON'T YOU, CHARLIE BROWN?

WELL, JUST TO SHOW YOU THAT I DO, I'VE FIGURED OUT A WAY FOR US TO PLAY NIGHT GAMES!

GO AHEAD... GO OUT ON THE PITCHER'S MOUND, AND SEE..

3-7

PEANUTS

THERE'S ANOTHER GOOD THING ABOUT PLAYING NIGHT GAMES, CHARLIE BROWN..

3-8

SAY YOU'RE PITCHING A LOUSY GAME, SEE, AND WE WANT TO GET YOU OUT OF THERE...WELL, ALL WE HAVE TO DO IS COME OUT TO THE MOUND AND BLOW OUT YOUR CANDLE!

POOF!

I THINK WE'D BETTER STICK TO DAY GAMES!

PEANUTS

IT'S KIND OF NICE NOT BEING MANAGER..

3-18

ON THE NIGHT BEFORE OUR GAMES I ALWAYS USED TO LIE AWAKE WORRYING...

I WONDER IF OUR NEW MANAGER IS LYING AWAKE WORRYING...

Z

PEANUTS

HEY, MANAGER, HOW COME WE NEVER TRY ANY FIELD GOALS?

I'M STANDING IN A FIELD, AREN'T I? HOW COME WE CAN'T TRY FOR A FIELD GOAL IF I'M STANDING IN A FIELD?

4-22

STUPID MANAGER!!!

PEANUTS

I DON'T WANT YOU TO HIT ANY OVER MY HEAD, DO YOU HEAR?

4-23

AND DON'T HIT ANY 'WAY OUT IN FRONT OF ME, EITHER! I WANT YOU TO HIT 'EM RIGHT TO ME!

BONK!

ALL RIGHT, THEN LET'S TRY HITTING 'EM A LITTLE TO ONE SIDE...

PEANUTS

PRACTICE?! WHY DO WE HAVE TO PRACTICE? WE NEVER WIN ANY GAMES...

4-24

WHAT ARE WE GONNA DO, PRACTICE OUR LOSING?!

THAT WAS JUST A LITTLE JOKE!

20

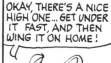

BEEETHOVEN

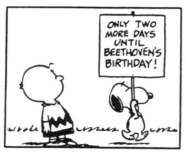

BIRDS

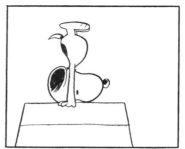

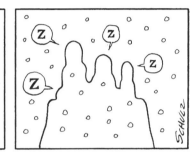

BLANKET

I CAN'T STAND THAT COMMERCIAL!

I'M DEPRESSED, LINUS...

I NEED AN ENCOURAGING WORD TO CHEER ME UP

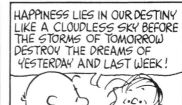

HAPPINESS LIES IN OUR DESTINY LIKE A CLOUDLESS SKY BEFORE THE STORMS OF TOMORROW DESTROY THE DREAMS OF YESTERDAY AND LAST WEEK!

I THINK THAT BLANKET IS DOING SOMETHING TO YOU!

YOU LIKE THAT BLANKET, DON'T YOU?

HOW MUCH DO YOU THINK IT IS WORTH?

WERE THIS BLANKET FROM THE FINEST SILKS OF PERSIA MADE, IT COULD NO MORE PRICELESS BE!

HOW POMPOUS CAN YOU GET?

BROTHERS

PEANUTS HEY, EVERYBODY! LET'S PLAY "KING OF THE HILL"!

WHOEVER IS ON TOP WILL BE "KING," SEE, AND...

ALL RIGHT, LET'S PLAY "QUEEN OF THE HILL"

PEANUTS I HAVE A MESSAGE FOR YOU...

MOM SAYS GET YOUR STUPID SELF IN THERE, AND CLEAN UP YOUR STUPID ROOM!

I'M SURE SHE DIDN'T SAY IT QUITE LIKE THAT

SO I ELABORATED A LITTLE..

PEANUTS 2-6

POOF!

PICK A CARD... ANY CARD..

BROTHERS

56

Strip 1 (5-14):
- YOU STUPID KID! YOU WOULDN'T SAY THAT IF MY BIG BROTHER WAS HERE!
- THEN AGAIN, MAYBE YOU WOULD!

Strip 2 (5-16):
- WHY DID I HAVE TO GET STUCK WITH A BIG BROTHER WHO'S A NOTHING?
- WHY AREN'T YOU THE HERO TYPE?
- WELL, I GUESS IF YOU'RE NOT THE HERO TYPE, YOU'RE JUST NOT THE HERO TYPE...
- DON'T GO QUOTING SHAKESPEARE TO ME!

Strip 3 (9-3):
- BOY, DID YOU EVER GOOF ME UP!
- YOU HAD ME TAKE MY LUNCH TO SCHOOL IN A LUNCH BOX ...DO YOU KNOW WHAT HAPPENED?
- ALL THE OTHER KIDS WERE BROWN-BAGGING IT!! I FELT LIKE A FOOL!
- YOU GAVE ME BAD ADVICE, BIG BROTHER!
- I CAN'T STAND ALL THIS RESPONSIBILITY..

Strip 4 (5-11):
- AN AQUARIUM? IT'S VERY NICE, BUT WHAT MADE YOU DECIDE TO BUY AN AQUARIUM?
- IT'S TIMELY! HAVEN'T YOU HEARD? THIS IS THE AGE OF AQUARIUMS!
- AQUARIUS
- WHAT?
- FORGET IT!
- BIG BROTHERS NEVER KNOW WHAT THEY'RE TALKING ABOUT

Title panel: **PEANUTS** featuring "Good ol' Charlie Brown" by Schulz

BOOT!

10-12

I LOST YOUR FOOTBALL, BIG BROTHER...I KICKED IT SO HIGH IT NEVER CAME DOWN..

DON'T WORRY ABOUT IT... IT'LL COME DOWN...

BIG BROTHERS KNOW EVERYTHING!

PEANUTS

A NEW BABY BROTHER! I CAN'T BELIEVE IT!

5-24

YOU MIGHT AS WELL COME BACK IN... I CAN'T FIGHT THE WHOLE WORLD

WHAT DO YOU MEAN BY THAT?

DAD JUST CALLED FROM THE HOSPITAL..WE HAVE A NEW BABY BROTHER!

A NEW BABY BROTHER!?

I THROW ONE OUT, AND ANOTHER COMES IN! YOU CAN'T SHOVEL WATER WITH A PITCHFORK

PEANUTS

C'MON, RERUN, I'M GOING TO TAKE YOU FOR A LITTLE WALK..

B2   3-26

IT'S ABOUT TIME YOU GOT A LOOK AT THE OUTSIDE WORLD

WELL, WHAT DO YOU THINK?

YOU MEAN THIS IS IT?

PEANUTS

CHARLIE BROWN, THIS IS MY BROTHER, "RERUN"...CAN HE BE ON OUR TEAM?

A LITTLE KID LIKE THAT?

HOW CAN HE HELP OUR TEAM?

3-29

HE DOESN'T SMOKE!

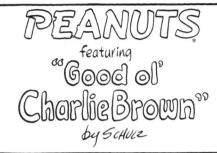

CAMP

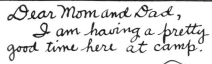

THE CAT
NEXT DOOR

SNARL!
SLASH!
GROWL!
SLASH!

THE CAT NEXT DOOR

76

HEY, CAT!

I DON'T APPRECIATE THE WAY YOU'VE BEEN SCRATCHING UP MY HOUSE! FROM NOW ON, KEEP YOUR CLAWS TO YOURSELF!!

RIP!

WELL, BETTER GET OUT THE OL' PUTTY KNIFE..

HEY, STUPID CAT... PUTTING ON A LITTLE WEIGHT, AREN'T YOU?

YOU SHOULD TAKE UP TENNIS... YOU ALREADY HAVE THE GUT!

SLASH!

AND A WICKED FOREHAND!

HEY, STUPID CAT, I'M SORT OF CURIOUS...

WHAT ARE YOU GOING TO GET ME FOR A WEDDING PRESENT?

POW

I WAS HOPING FOR A SET OF BUTTER KNIVES

HEY, STUPID CAT! YOU WERE OUT KIND OF LATE LAST NIGHT, WEREN'T YOU? WHAT WERE YOU DOING, STAR GAZING?

NO, YOU'RE SO STUPID YOU PROBABLY DON'T EVEN KNOW WHAT A STAR LOOKS LIKE!
HEE HEE HEE

SLASH

✿ ✿
SNARL!
SLASH!
GROWL!
SLASH!
✿ ✿

HEY, STUPID CAT!

I'M NOT AFRAID OF YOU ANY MORE..

IF YOU COME NEAR ME AGAIN, YOU KNOW WHAT I'LL DO?

I'LL HIT YOU WITH MY SANDWICH!

SOMEHOW I HAVE THE FEELING YOU'RE TRYING TO GET SOMETHING FROM ME

YOU'RE AFTER LINUS'S BLANKET, AREN'T YOU? WELL, I DON'T HAVE IT!

I GAVE IT TO THAT KITTY NEXT DOOR

KITTY?!

SOME KITTY!

✿ ✿
SNARL! SLASH! GROWL! SLASH!
✿ ✿

EUDORA GAVE MY BLANKET TO THE CAT NEXT DOOR?!

WELL, GET IT BACK!!

YOU'RE NOT AFRAID OF A CAT, ARE YOU?

I AM WHEN HE WEIGHS TWO HUNDRED THOUSAND POUNDS!

DANCING

YOU WOULDN'T BE SO HAPPY IF YOU KNEW ABOUT ALL THE TROUBLES IN THIS WORLD!

DON'T TELL ME... I DON'T WANT TO KNOW...

I'M OUTRAGEOUSLY HAPPY IN MY STUPIDITY!

I DON'T UNDERSTAND YOU!

THE WHOLE WORLD IS COMING APART, AND YOU'RE DANCING!

I CAN'T HELP IT... MY FEET LOVE TO DANCE...

I HAVE AN OBLIGATION TO MY FEET!

YOU'RE NOT AS HAPPY AS YOU THINK YOU ARE!

NOBODY COULD BE THAT HAPPY!

PERHAPS SHE'S RIGHT...

ON THE OTHER HAND, MAYBE I'VE SET A NEW RECORD!

HAPPINESS IS HAVING YOUR DOG COME HOME!

AMEN!

DOG

I WOULD HAVE MADE A GOOD PRAIRIE DOG!

THERE'S A PRAIRIE DOG IN OUR BACK YARD

PRAIRIE DOGS WENT OUT WITH THE COVERED WAGON

LUCY SAYS PRAIRIE DOGS WENT OUT WITH THE COVERED WAGON

WE PRAIRIE DOGS ARE MAKING A COME BACK!

WELL, HOW WAS YOUR VACATION, CHARLIE BROWN?

VACATIONS ARE DREADED, SUFFERED, ENDURED, TOLERATED, SPOILED, RUINED AND WASTED...

VACATIONS CAN BE GREAT, TERRIBLE, WONDERFUL, AWFUL, DELIGHTFUL AND STUPID

I SPENT MY WHOLE VACATION WORRYING ABOUT MY DOG..

YOU NEED A VACATION, CHARLIE BROWN!

HAPPINESS IS HAVING YOUR DOG COME HOME!

AMEN!

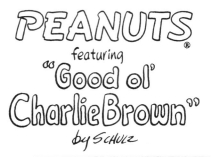

PEANUTS

Dear Dog, This is to inform you that you are one of the finalists for this year's Daisy Hill Puppy Cup Award.

THE DAISY HILL PUPPY CUP!! I'VE BEEN NOMINATED FOR THE DAISY HILL PUPPY CUP!!!

WHEEEEEE!

STUPID BEAGLE!

2-27

PEANUTS

SO THE DAISY HILL PUPPY CUP IS AWARDED TO THE OUTSTANDING NEIGHBORHOOD DOG OF THE YEAR..

YOU'RE GOING TO HAVE SOME PRETTY STRONG COMPETITION

3-1

WHAT MAKES YOU THINK YOU CAN WIN?

I'M SO CUTE!

PEANUTS

HERE ARE SOME MORE RULES ABOUT THE DAISY HILL PUPPY CUP AWARD

"EACH NOMINEE MUST SUBMIT FIVE LETTERS FROM INTERESTED PARTIES STATING WHY HE SHOULD BE NAMED 'THE NEIGHBORHOOD DOG OF THE YEAR'"

3-2

DON'T ASK **ME** TO WRITE A LETTER FOR YOU! I WOULDN'T RECOMMEND YOU FOR "DOG OF THE MINUTE"!

WHAAH!

AND CRYING WON'T HELP!!

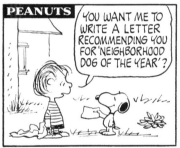

PEANUTS

He is truly a good dog.

type type type

He is also a loyal friend.

Therefore, I would like to recommend ol' banana nose for Neighborhood Dog of the Year.

3-10

HEE HEE HEE HEE HEE HEE

ARGGH!!

PEANUTS

I THINK THEY'RE GOING TO ANNOUNCE THE WINNER OF THE DAISY HILL PUPPY CUP TOMORROW

DOES SNOOPY THINK HE HAS A CHANCE? IS HE CONFIDENT?

OH, YES... HE'S VERY CONFIDENT..

3-12

WHY ELSE WOULD HE BE BUILDING A TROPHY CASE?

PEANUTS

THEY'VE ANNOUNCED THE WINNER...

DID I WIN? DID I WIN? TELL ME I WON! DID I WIN?

YOU DIDN'T WIN!

AAUGH!

I HATE THE WORLD! I HATE EVERYBODY AND EVERYTHING IN THE WHOLE STUPID WORLD-WIDE WORLD!!

3-14

THERE'S NOTHING LIKE A GOOD LOSER

EASTER BEAGLE

EASTER BEAGLE

104

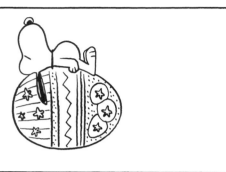

4-22

107

FISHING

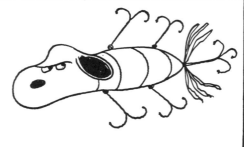

PEANUTS

WHAT ARE YOU FISHING FOR, COMPLIMENTS?

HA HA HA HA HA HA HA!

I HATE JOKES LIKE THAT!

YOU'RE GOING TO TAKE ME FISHING? THAT'S GREAT! I DON'T KNOW ANYTHING ABOUT FISHING

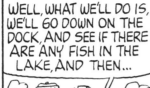

WELL, WHAT WE'LL DO IS, WE'LL GO DOWN ON THE DOCK, AND SEE IF THERE ARE ANY FISH IN THE LAKE, AND THEN...

I SEE ONE!

YOU JUST PADDLE AROUND THERE AWHILE, AND I'LL EXPLAIN ABOUT THESE POLES...

OKAY, EUDORA, YOU FISH IN THIS PART OF THE STREAM, AND I'LL FISH DOWN THERE IN THAT PART...

I DON'T THINK THIS IS GOING TO WORK

WHAT'S THE TROUBLE?

EITHER THE STREAM IS TOO NARROW, OR MY LINE IS TOO LONG...

THANK YOU FOR TEACHING ME ABOUT FISHING TODAY, SALLY... I HAD FUN!

I EVEN WROTE HOME TO MY DAD, AND TOLD HIM THAT I CAUGHT A BLUE MARLIN...

GOOD GRIEF! HE'LL NEVER BELIEVE A STORY LIKE THAT!

HE'LL BELIEVE IT... HE WANTS ME TO BE HAPPY...

6-13

I'VE NEVER HEARD OF ANYONE FISHING IN THE SNOW...

1-26

I CAN'T IMAGINE WHAT YOU EXPECT TO CATCH...

SNOWFISH!

FISHING FOR COMPLIMENTS?

THAT'S THE DUMBEST THING I'VE EVER HEARD!!

5-25

"YOU'RE SWEET...YOU HAVE NICE EYES...YOU'RE KIND OF CUTE...YOU HAVE A GREAT BOD..."

FIVE CENTS PLEASE!

PEANUTS

PSYCHIATRIC HELP 5¢

THE DOCTOR IS [IN]

I DON'T KNOW WHAT TO DO...

SOMETIMES I GET SO LONELY I CAN HARDLY STAND IT...

OTHER TIMES, I ACTUALLY LONG TO BE COMPLETELY ALONE...

TRY TO LIVE IN-BETWEEN... FIVE CENTS, PLEASE!

THE DOCTOR IS [IN]

5-30

PEANUTS

PSYCHIATRIC HELP 5¢

THE DOCTOR IS [IN]

WHAT CAN YOU DO FOR SOMEONE WHO IS IN "REJECTION-SLIP SHOCK"?

TELL HIM THAT WHAT HE HAS WRITTEN IS JUST AS GOOD AS A LOT OF OTHER THINGS YOU SEE BEING PUBLISHED THESE DAYS...

WHAT YOU HAVE WRITTEN, SNOOPY, IS JUST AS GOOD AS A LOT OF OTHER THINGS YOU SEE BEING PUBLISHED THESE DAYS...

9-13

CHIATRIC HELP 5¢

THE DOCTOR IS [IN]

FIVE CENTS, PLEASE..

WHERE AM I? WHAT HAPPENED?

SCHULZ

PEANUTS

PSYCHIATR HELP 5¢

THE DOCTOR IS [IN]

YOU PAID NINE DOLLARS TO SIT NEXT TO YOUR HERO AT A SPORTS BANQUET, AND HE DIDN'T SHOW UP?

NOT ONLY THAT, LAST WEEK I WENT SKIING, AND FELL OFF THE CHAIR-LIFT!

1-3

I'VE COME TO YOU FOR A WORD OF ENCOURAGEMENT

THE DOCTOR IS [IN]

HAPPY NEW YEAR... FIVE CENTS, PLEASE!

THE DOCTOR IS [IN]

SCHULZ

FIVE CENTS PLEASE!

GOLF

PEANUTS

HERE'S THE WORLD FAMOUS GOLF-PRO RECEIVING HIS INVITATION TO PLAY IN THE MASTERS

4-8

AH, WHAT A THRILL !! GEORGIA IN THE SPRING!

I CAN SEE MYSELF NOW STANDING ON THE FIRST TEE...

ACTUALLY, BEAGLES ARE ALMOST NEVER INVITED TO PLAY IN THE MASTERS...

PEANUTS

HERE'S THE WORLD FAMOUS GOLF PRO GOING OUT TO PLAY A PRACTICE ROUND AT THE MASTERS

4-10

I'LL PROBABLY PLAY WITH ARNIE TODAY, OR SAM, OR BEN, OR GAY...

OF COURSE, THEY DON'T ALWAYS LIKE TO PLAY WITH ME...

THEY HATE IT WHEN I OUTDRIVE THEM!

PEANUTS

HERE'S THE WORLD FAMOUS GOLF PRO TEEING OFF ON THE FIRST HOLE AT THE MASTERS...

4-11

AS HE WALKS DOWN THE FIRST FAIRWAY, HE IS FOLLOWED BY THAT HUGE THRONG OF HIS ADMIRERS KNOWN AS "SNOOPY'S SQUAD"

WINTER RULES ?

PEANUTS

IT'S THE SECOND DAY OF THE BIG MASTERS GOLF TOURNAMENT IN AUGUSTA, GEORGIA..

4-12

NO MOVIE CAMERAS, PLEASE!

HERE'S THE WORLD-FAMOUS GOLF PRO LINING UP HIS PUTT ON THE SIXTEENTH GREEN........

PEANUTS

4-27

I HATE THESE PAR FIVES THAT YOU CAN'T REACH IN FORTY-TWO

PEANUTS

WHAT ARE YOU DOING HOME?

I THOUGHT YOU WERE IN AUGUSTA PLAYING IN THE MASTERS GOLF TOURNAMENT.. DIDN'T YOU MAKE THE CUT?

4-13

HOW COME YOU'RE NOT PLAYING IN THE FINAL ROUND?

WELL, I RAN INTO THIS CUTE LITTLE GEORGIA BEAGLE, SEE...

PEANUTS

MY DAD IS KIND OF A PHILOSOPHER..

HE SAYS THAT THE GAME OF GOLF AND THE GAME OF LIFE ARE VERY SIMILAR...

THAT'S TRUE

UNFORTUNATELY, IN THE GAME OF LIFE, I'M ALWAYS HITTING FROM THE BACK TEES!

PEANUTS

MY DAD SAYS THAT LIFE IS LIKE A GAME OF GOLF

DO YOU THINK HE'S RIGHT?

ABSOLUTELY

AND I FEEL LIKE I'VE JUST BOGEYED THE LAST FIVE HOLES!

PEANUTS

Immediately after he won the golf tournament, he was interviewed on TV.

"This is the most exciting moment of my life!" he said.

"I saw you on TV," said his wife. "I thought the day we got married was the most exciting moment of your life."

In his next tournament, he failed to make the cut.

GOOD GRIEF, DON'T GO OUT OF BOUNDS!

4-6

HIT A TREE! HIT A BUILDING!

HIT A HOUSEWIFE!

CADDIES, HUH?

OKAY, YOU'RE JUST IN TIME... MRS. BARTLEY AND MRS. NELSON WERE LOOKING FOR CADDIES

6-18

HE SAID TO GRAB THEIR CLUBS, AND GET OUT TO THE FIRST TEE, MARCIE...

I THINK WE'RE IN TROUBLE, SIR!

GOOD GOING, MARCIE, YOU MADE IT TO THE FIRST TEE...

HERE'S YOUR DRIVER, MRS. NELSON...

6-21

MARCIE, HAND MRS. BARTLEY HER DRIVER!

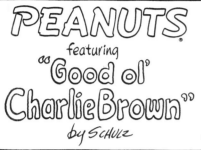

GOOD GRIEF!

140

PEANUTS
featuring
"Good ol' CharlieBrown"
by SCHULZ

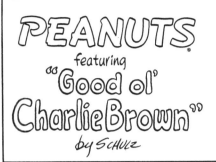

DOG FOR SALE

DO YOU THINK PETS ARE IMPORTANT?

SURE

A FRIEND OF MINE AT SCHOOL GOT SOME GOLDFISH FOR HIS BIRTHDAY, BUT I DON'T THINK HE REALLY WANTED THEM..

PEOPLE BUY PETS FOR STRANGE REASONS

HOW DID YOU HAPPEN TO GET SNOOPY, CHARLIE BROWN?

WELL, I'M NOT QUITE SURE BECAUSE I WAS KIND OF YOUNG..

I THINK IT STARTED BECAUSE OF SOMETHING THAT HAPPENED AT A PLAYGROUND... I WAS PLAYING IN A SANDBOX WITH A COUPLE OF OTHER KIDS...I CAN'T EVEN REMEMBER WHO THEY WERE...

ANYWAY, ALL OF A SUDDEN, ONE OF THEM POURED A WHOLE BUCKET OF SAND OVER MY HEAD...I STARTED CRYING, I GUESS, AND MY MOTHER CAME RUNNING UP, AND TOOK ME HOME

IT'S KIND OF EMBARRASSING NOW TO TALK ABOUT IT

ANYWAY, THE NEXT DAY WE DROVE OUT TO THE DAISY HILL PUPPY FARM, AND MY MOTHER AND DAD BOUGHT ME A DOG...

GOOD GRIEF!

SCHULZ

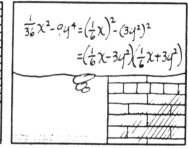

PEANUTS

I ORDERED A TOY BICYCLE FOR YOUR DOLL SET, BUT IT NEVER CAME...

I HAVE A FEELING IT WAS PROBABLY DELIVERED TO THE WRONG ADDRESS...

WELL, I HOPE WHOEVER GOT IT, ENJOYS IT!!

12-28

WHEELIES, YET! GOOD GRIEF!

PEANUTS

THE BURGLARS ARE COMING BACK!

I CAN HEAR THEM IN THE LIVING ROOM! THEY'RE STEALING ALL OUR FURNITURE!

DO SOMETHING, SNOOPY! SCARE THEM OFF! BARK AT THEM!!!

1-25

GURGLE!

OH, GOOD GRIEF!

CHARLES, WHAT'S A "GOOSE EGG"?

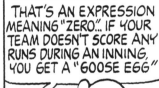

THAT'S AN EXPRESSION MEANING "ZERO"... IF YOUR TEAM DOESN'T SCORE ANY RUNS DURING AN INNING, YOU GET A "GOOSE EGG"

3-30

THAT'S IT!

WHAT?

THAT'LL BE THE NAME OF OUR TEAM..."THE GOOSE EGGS"!

OH, GOOD GRIEF!

PEANUTS

English Report – "Familiar Quotations"

12-30

My favorite "Familiar Quotation" is "Drop Dead!"

It is a very useful quotation. It can be used for almost any occasion.

GOOD GRIEF!

DROP DEAD!!

THE GREAT PUMPKIN

PEANUTS

HELLO?

HELLO, LUCILLE? THIS IS PEPPERMINT PATTY...SAY, I'M CALLING ABOUT A PECULIAR LETTER I GOT FROM YOUR BROTHER...IT HAS TO DO WITH A "GREAT PUMPKIN"

10-18

I SEE...WELL, LINUS IS GOING BY RIGHT NOW...DO YOU WANT TO TALK TO HIM?

HERE HE IS!

STOMP

PEANUTS

OKAY, LINUS, TELL ME ALL ABOUT THE "GREAT PUMPKIN"

WELL, IT'S LIKE THIS...

ON HALLOWEEN NIGHT, THE "GREAT PUMPKIN" CHOOSES THE PUMPKIN PATCH THAT HE THINKS IS THE MOST SINCERE... THEN HE RISES OUT OF THE PUMPKIN PATCH, AND FLIES THROUGH THE AIR BRINGING PRESENTS TO CHILDREN EVERYWHERE

10-24

I BELIEVE YOU!

YOU DO?!

FANTASTIC!

PEANUTS

IF YOU'RE LOOKING FOR CHARLIE BROWN, I DON'T THINK HE'S HOME

I WONDER IF I SHOULD WAIT...

WHY NOT? BY THE WAY, MY NAME IS LINUS...

10-17

HI... I'M FRANKLIN..

I'M VERY GLAD TO KNOW YOU

WHILE WE'RE WAITING, WOULD YOU LIKE TO HEAR A FEW WORDS ABOUT THE "GREAT PUMPKIN"?

PEANUTS

Dear Great Pumpkin, Once again I look to your arrival.

I shall be sitting in my sincere pumpkin patch waiting for you. I have been good all year.

I'M NOT A HYPOCRITE!

I NEVER SAID A WORD...

I THOUGHT YOU WERE GOING TO CALL ME A HYPOCRITE..

HOW SENSITIVE CAN YOU GET?

PEANUTS

I BELIEVE THAT THE "GREAT PUMPKIN" WILL RISE FROM THE PUMPKIN PATCH ON HALLOWEEN NIGHT

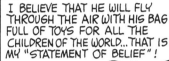

I BELIEVE THAT HE WILL FLY THROUGH THE AIR WITH HIS BAG FULL OF TOYS FOR ALL THE CHILDREN OF THE WORLD...THAT IS MY "STATEMENT OF BELIEF"!

HERE COMES CHARLIE BROWN... REPEAT FOR HIM YOUR "STATEMENT OF STUPIDITY"

THAT'S "BELIEF"!!

EXCUSE ME..

PEANUTS

TOMORROW IS HALLOWEEN, SNOOPY..

TOMORROW NIGHT I'LL BE SITTING HERE IN THIS SINCERE PUMPKIN PATCH, AND I'LL SEE THE 'GREAT PUMPKIN'! HE'LL COME FLYING THROUGH THE AIR, AND I'LL BE HERE TO SEE HIM!

ISN'T THAT EXCITING?

WHEE!

PEANUTS

IT'S NINE O'CLOCK..

GRAMMA SAYS AS LONG AS SHE IS BABY-SITTING, SHE WANTS YOU TO COME IN NOW...

DOESN'T SHE KNOW TONIGHT IS HALLOWEEN? DOESN'T SHE KNOW I'M WAITING FOR THE 'GREAT PUMPKIN'? I CAN'T GO IN NOW!!

GRAMMA SAYS TO STOP ALL THIS NONSENSE, AND COME IN RIGHT NOW!!!

AAUGH!

FORGIVE HER, 'GREAT PUMPKIN'... SHE'S A VICTIM OF THE GENERATION GAP...

PEANUTS

WELL, DID YOU SEE THE 'GREAT PUMPKIN' LAST NIGHT?

HA!

ALL I SAW WAS MY BEDROOM! GRAMMA WAS BABY-SITTING, AND SHE WOULDN'T LET ME STAY OUT IN THE PUMPKIN PATCH...

SHE MADE YOU COME IN? I DON'T UNDERSTAND...

WHERE THE 'GREAT PUMPKIN' IS CONCERNED, GRAMMA IS VERY UPTIGHT!

PEANUTS

Dear Great Pumpkin, I am looking forward to your arrival on Halloween night.

SANTA CLAUS HAS ELVES TO HELP HIM.. WHAT DOES THE GREAT PUMPKIN HAVE, ORANGES?

HA HA HA HA!!!

Don't listen, sir. Lately, her kind is everywhere.

PEANUTS

THIS IS WHAT I BELIEVE..

I BELIEVE THAT THE GREAT PUMPKIN RISES OUT OF THE PUMPKIN PATCH ON HALLOWEEN NIGHT AND FLIES THROUGH THE AIR, BRINGING WITH HIM TOYS FOR ALL THE CHILDREN IN THE WORLD!

THAT'S WHAT I BELIEVE... WHAT DO YOU THINK?

I THINK YOU HAVE VERY NICE EYES, AND YOU ARE COMPLETELY OUT OF YOUR MIND!

HALLOWEEN IS OVER..

HAVE YOU BEEN SITTING OUT IN THAT PUMPKIN PATCH ALL NIGHT AGAIN?

I WAS WAITING FOR THE GREAT PUMPKIN...HE DIDN'T COME..

WHY DON'T YOU JUST CURSE THE GREAT PUMPKIN, AND FORGET THE WHOLE THING?

YOU SOUND LIKE JOB'S WIFE

SHAKE YOUR FIST IN THE AIR, AND SAY, "CURSE YOU, GREAT PUMPKIN! I KNOW YOU DON'T EXIST!"

THEN YOU'D BE FREE! YOU CAN DO IT!!

JUST SAY, "CURSE YOU, GREAT PUMPKIN! I KNOW YOU DON'T EXIST! I DON'T NEED YOU! I'M FREE! I'M FREE!"

COME ON, YOU CAN DO IT! JUST SAY IT!

COME ON! SAY IT!

JUST WAIT 'TIL NEXT YEAR!!

OH, GOOD GRIEF!

PEANUTS

SIR, WHAT IN THE WORLD ARE YOU DOING SITTING IN A PUMPKIN PATCH?

HALLOWEEN IS COMING, MARCIE.. LINUS TOLD ME THAT ON HALLOWEEN NIGHT THE "GREAT PUMPKIN" RISES OUT OF THE PUMPKIN PATCH, AND BRINGS GIFTS TO ALL THE KIDS IN THE WORLD!

10-23

DO YOU REALLY BELIEVE THAT, SIR?

I HAVE TO BELIEVE IT, MARCIE...

I'M IN BAD NEED OF A NEW BASEBALL GLOVE!

SCHULZ

PEANUTS

YOU THINK NO ONE BELIEVES IN THE "GREAT PUMPKIN," DON'T YOU?

WELL, PEPPERMINT PATTY DOES! RIGHT THIS MOMENT SHE'S SITTING IN A PUMPKIN PATCH WAITING FOR THE "GREAT PUMPKIN" TO APPEAR!

SHE'S NOT LIKE YOU! SHE DOESN'T CALL THE "GREAT PUMPKIN" A MYTH AND A LEGEND!

10-25

HOW ABOUT A LIE AND A FRAUD?

SCHULZ

PEANUTS

TODAY IS VETERAN'S DAY, LINUS...

DO YOU THINK IT'S WRONG TO BE SITTING IN A PUMPKIN PATCH WAITING FOR THE "GREAT PUMPKIN" ON VETERAN'S DAY?

10-27

NO, I DON'T THINK SO... I HAVE A FEELING THAT THE VETERANS WOULD UNDERSTAND

THE BEST WAY TO CELEBRATE, OF COURSE, IS TO GO OVER TO BILL MAULDIN'S HOUSE, AND QUAFF A FEW ROOT BEERS!

SCHULZ

PEANUTS

YOU'RE GOING TO BE SO EXCITED, PATTY...

10-28

WHEN THE "GREAT PUMPKIN" RISES OUT OF THE PUMPKIN PATCH ON HALLOWEEN NIGHT, IT'S A SIGHT TO BEHOLD!

DOES THIS PUMPKIN PATCH LOOK SINCERE ENOUGH, LINUS?

DON'T ASK!! ONLY THE "GREAT PUMPKIN" CAN MAKE THAT JUDGMENT!

WOW!!

SCHULZ

PEANUTS

TOMORROW NIGHT IS HALLOWEEN

I DON'T SUPPOSE YOU'D CARE TO HAVE ME TELL YOU ALL ABOUT THE "GREAT PUMPKIN"??

NO, I WOULDN'T CARE FOR THAT AT ALL

WOULD YOU READ ONE OF OUR PAMPHLETS?

10-30

WELL, ANOTHER HALLOWEEN HAS COME AND GONE

DID YOU EVER SEE THE "GREAT PUMPKIN"?

NO, AND I JUST DON'T UNDERSTAND IT...

11-1

I THOUGHT MARCIE WAS WITH YOU... WHAT HAPPENED TO MARCIE?

HER PARENTS CAME AND GOT HER...SHE'S BEING DEPROGRAMMED!

MY FAMILY SAID IT'S ALL RIGHT TO BELIEVE IN SANTA CLAUS, BUT NOT THE GREAT PUMPKIN

11-3

THEY SAID YOU WERE A FALSE PROPHET

WHAT ELSE?

THAT'S ALL.. NOTHING ELSE...

WHAT ELSE?

WELL, THEY ALSO SAID YOU WERE CRAZY..

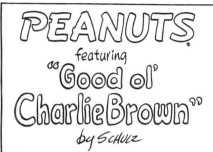

HERE WE ARE...

NOW, THIS WILL BE SORT OF A REHEARSAL FOR TOMORROW NIGHT, SNOOPY...

TOMORROW IS HALLOWEEN, AND ON HALLOWEEN NIGHT THE GREAT PUMPKIN RISES OUT OF THE PUMPKIN PATCH, AND BRINGS TOYS TO ALL THE CHILDREN IN THE WORLD...

YOUR JOB IS TO BE KIND OF A PAUL REVERE...WHEN THE GREAT PUMPKIN COMES, YOU'LL GET ON YOUR HORSE, AND RIDE THROUGH THE COUNTRYSIDE SPREADING THE NEWS!

OKAY, LET'S REHEARSE IT..

HE'S COMING! HE'S COMING! THE GREAT PUMPKIN IS COMING!

RIDE, SNOOPY, RIDE! SPREAD THE NEWS!

I FEEL LIKE SUCH A FOOL!

10-30

ICE

CREAM

PEANUTS

THAT DIDN'T REALLY BOTHER ME...IF YOU EXPECT NOTHING, YOU GET NOTHING...

8-9   SCHULZ

PEANUTS

YOU UNDERSTAND THAT I'M NOT JUST RUSHING OFF, DON'T YOU?

OF COURSE, I UNDERSTAND..SO GET GOING! IT'S IMPORTANT!

8-18

I'D RUSH OFF, TOO, IF I JUST REMEMBERED THAT I'D LEFT AN ICE CREAM CONE IN THE GLOVE COMPARTMENT OF MY DAD'S CAR!

SCHULZ

PEANUTS   2-20

THUMB À LA MODE!

SCHULZ

PEANUTS

ALL RIGHT, SWITCH CHANNELS!

AND GET UP SO I CAN SIT THERE!

WHILE YOU'RE UP, GO INTO THE KITCHEN AND GET ME SOME ICE CREAM!

I'M SURPRISED THAT MY HAIR DOESN'T TURN GRAY..

5-18   SCHULZ

IT WAS A DARK AND STORMY NIGHT

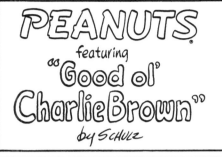

JOE

COOL

PEANUTS

HERE'S JOE COOL HANGING AROUND THE STUDENT UNION

5-27

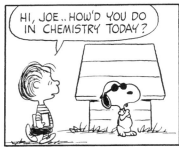

HI, JOE.. HOW'D YOU DO IN CHEMISTRY TODAY?

THAT CHEMISTRY IS A DRAG, MAN

JOE COOL CAN'T WORRY ABOUT CHEMISTRY WHEN HE'S BUSY HANGING AROUND THE STUDENT UNION

SCHULZ

PEANUTS

HERE'S JOE COOL HANGING AROUND THE DORM ON A SATURDAY AFTERNOON

HI, JOE

WHAT ARE YOU DOING HANGING AROUND THE DORM ON A SATURDAY AFTERNOON?

5-29

NO WHEELS, MAN!

SCHULZ

PEANUTS

HERE'S JOE COOL HANGING AROUND THE STUDENT UNION EYEING CHICKS

5-28

ACTUALLY, WE JOE COOLS ARE SCARED TO DEATH OF CHICKS

SCHULZ

PEANUTS

HERE'S JOE COOL LOOKING OVER A FEW OF THE LANGUAGE COURSES FOR THIS TERM

9-22

I'M VERY HUNG-UP ON LANGUAGES... MAYBE I'LL STUDY HEBREW AND KOREAN AND SERBIAN...

HI, JOE... I SEE YOU'RE DOWN FOR BONEHEAD ENGLISH AGAIN...

※ SIGH ※

PEANUTS   11-24

NO ONE EVER INVITES JOE COOL HOME FOR THANKSGIVING...

PEANUTS

HERE'S JOE COOL HANGING AROUND THE CAMPUS ON THANKSGIVING DAY..

EVERYTHING IS CLOSED... EVERYONE HAS GONE HOME... NO CHICKS... NOTHING!

NO ONE INVITED JOE COOL HOME FOR THANKSGIVING SO HE'S BUYING A HAMBURGER AND A MALT AT A DRIVE-IN...

11-25

BLEAH!

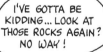

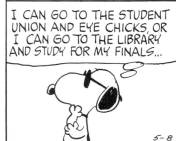

PEANUTS

SO YOUR SISTER THREW YOU OUT OF THE HOUSE..

YES, I'M LIVING HERE IN THE DORM WITH JOE COOL

IS IT COMFORTABLE? HOW'S THE FOOD? WHERE DO YOU EAT?

I DON'T KNOW.. I SUPPOSE WE EAT IN THE CAMPUS CAFETERIA

NO WAY! JOE COOL ALWAYS SENDS OUT FOR A PIZZA!

PEANUTS

♡ HI, ♡ SWEETIE!

HI, JOE...WHO'S YOUR FRIEND WITH THE BLANKET?

THAT'S A GOOD QUESTION..

OUR DORM GETS ALL THE STRANGE ONES!

PEANUTS

HI!

GO AWAY.. YOU DON'T LIVE HERE ANY MORE!

I WAS JUST CHECKING

WHO'S YOUR FRIEND?

OH, THIS IS JOE COOL.. WE LIVE IN THE SAME DORM

I THINK YOU'RE BOTH OUT OF YOUR MIND!

YOU GET THAT WAY WHEN YOU LIVE IN A DORM TOO LONG..

PEANUTS

SAY, JOE, I'VE BEEN WANTING TO ASK YOU..

HOW COME YOU NEVER GO TO ANY CLASSES?

CLASSES ?!

THOSE CLASSES CAN RUIN YOUR GRADE AVERAGE!

WHY COULDN'T SHE JUST STAY AWAY?

WHY DID SHE HAVE TO COME BACK?

POOCHIE, IT'S GOOD TO SEE YOU AFTER ALL THESE YEARS..

WHERE'S SNOOPY?

YOU WERE THE ONE WHO FIRST STARTED TO CALL ME CHARLIE BROWN...

I WONDER IF SNOOPY WILL REMEMBER ME...

HE'S CHANGED A LITTLE SINCE YOU LIVED AROUND HERE...

HE'S PROBABLY OUT IN THE BACK YARD AND...

I'M REALLY ANXIOUS TO SEE HIM...I REMEMBER WHAT A CUTE LITTLE PUPPY HE WAS...

SNOOPY?

SNOOPY, WHERE ARE YOU? SNOOPY?

!

THOMAS WOLFE WAS RIGHT...YOU CAN'T GO HOME AGAIN!

PEANUTS

HERE'S JOE COOL RETURNING TO THE DORM AFTER A NIGHT OUT WITH THE GUYS...

10-6

IT'S GOOD TO GET AWAY FROM THE BOOKS ONCE IN AWHILE

Z

HE CLIMBS THE STAIRS TO THE SECOND FLOOR OF THE DORM...

AND QUICKLY PASSES OUT FROM DRINKING TOO MUCH ROOT BEER!

SCHULZ

HERE'S JOE COOL HANGING AROUND THE BULLETIN BOARD

9-13

THIS IS A GREAT WAY TO MEET SOME REALLY NEAT CHICKS

OF COURSE, SOME OF THEM THINK THEY'RE PRETTY SMART...

SCHULZ

PEANUTS

HERE'S JOE COOL HANGING AROUND THE DORM...

JOE COOL ALWAYS KEEPS UP WITH THE LATEST CAMPUS FADS...

5-6

AND WHAT'S THE LATEST CAMPUS FAD?

STREAKING!!!

SCHULZ

KITES

I GIVE UP!! I'LL NEVER GET THIS KITE IN THE AIR!

WHY COULDN'T I HAVE BEEN OWNED BY SOME KINDLY OLD RANCHER IN WYOMING?

LETTERS

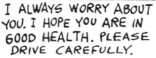

PEANUTS

IT'S A CHAIN LETTER, SEE, AND IF YOU SEND SIX COPIES TO SIX FRIENDS, YOU GET GOOD LUCK!

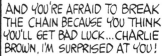

AND YOU'RE AFRAID TO BREAK THE CHAIN BECAUSE YOU THINK YOU'LL GET BAD LUCK...CHARLIE BROWN, I'M SURPRISED AT YOU!

WHAT SORT OF WORLD WOULD THIS BE IF A PERSON'S DESTINY COULD BE CONTROLLED BY SUCH A STUPID THING AS A CHAIN LETTER?

WHAT ABOUT THAT BLANKET YOU DRAG AROUND?

DON'T GET PERSONAL!

PEANUTS

I REFUSE TO LET A STUPID CHAIN LETTER DOMINATE MY LIFE!

I'M GOING TO DEFY BAD LUCK! I'M GOING TO RIP THIS LETTER TO SHREDS, AND NEVER ANSWER IT!

I'M FREE!!

PEANUTS

I'M WRITING A LAST-MINUTE LETTER TO SANTA CLAUS...

I SEE...

MISTAKE!

THIS IS GOING TO BE A BAD CHRISTMAS..

ALL MY LETTERS TO SANTA CLAUS CAME BACK UNOPENED!

12-13

Dear Santa Claus, You can't bluff me.

I know that you are wishy washy. I know that you will bring me presents whether I'm good or whether I am bad.

US MAIL

INTO THE TEETH OF THE STORM!

US MAIL

12-22

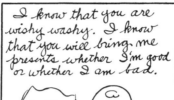

HERE, SNOOPY, YOU GOT A LETTER..

A MYSTERIOUS LETTER!

MY PEACEFUL LIFE HAS BEEN INTERRUPTED BY THE UNEXPLAINED ARRIVAL OF A MYSTERIOUS LETTER

IT'S PROBABLY BAD NEWS... EITHER THAT OR GOOD NEWS..

I LOVE MYSTERIOUS LETTERS!

1-5

WELL, WHO'S THE MYSTERIOUS LETTER FROM?

OOOOooo!

KLUNK!

HE FAINTED!

WHAT ELSE?

WHEN YOU RECEIVE A LETTER FROM THE HEAD BEAGLE, YOU ALWAYS FAINT!

1-6

"Our love is different," she cried. "It will endure forever."

AH! MY SECRETARY WITH THE MORNING MAIL...

Dear Contributor,
Thank you for submitting your manuscript. We regret that it does not suit our present needs.

ANOTHER REJECTION SLIP...

RATS!

7-4

OH, WELL, TAKE IT AND FILE IT WITH THE OTHERS...

MOVIES

PEANUTS
featuring
"Good ol' Charlie Brown"
by SCHULZ

ONE, PLEASE...

WHAT'S THE NAME OF THIS MOVIE, LINUS?

IT'S CALLED "FEET"

IT'S ABOUT SOME FEET THAT TRAMPLE EVERYBODY, AND TAKE OVER THE WORLD

THAT SOUNDS GROSS...MAYBE I SHOULDN'T SEE IT...IF IT'S REALLY GROSS, I'LL FLIP OUT FOR SURE!

SUIT YOURSELF... ONE, PLEASE!

WHAT ARE YOU DOING HOME? I THOUGHT YOU WENT TO THE SHOW...

IT SOUNDED TOO SCARY... I DIDN'T GO IN...

THERE'S A GOOD ONE STARTING NEXT WEEK..IT'S CALLED "ELBOWS," AND IT'S ABOUT THESE GIANT ELBOWS WHO TAKE OVER THE UNIVERSE...

11-9

I THINK I'LL STAY IN BED NEXT WEEK

MUSIC

NEEEDLES

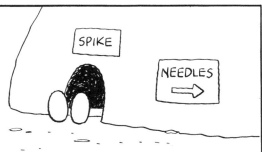

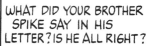

WHAT DID YOUR BROTHER SPIKE SAY IN HIS LETTER? IS HE ALL RIGHT?

HE SAYS HE FEELS SORT OF LONELY AND ANXIOUS...

BUT HE'S FOUND SOMEONE TO TALK TO, AND THAT SEEMS TO HELP..

I HAD THIS STRANGE DREAM LAST NIGHT...

I COME FROM A FAMILY OF EIGHT... AT FIRST, WE WERE QUITE CLOSE...

THINGS HAPPEN, AS YOU KNOW, AND MOST OF US GRADUALLY LOST TOUCH...

I CAN'T BELIEVE I'M SITTING IN THE MIDDLE OF THE DESERT TALKING TO A CACTUS!

I SHOULD GO INTO NEEDLES TONIGHT.. I CAN SEE THE BRIGHT LIGHTS BECKONING ME...

MAYBE I'D SEE A CUTE CHICK, AND I'D SAY TO HER, "HEY, HOW'D YOU LIKE TO GO PLAY VIDEO GAMES?"

JUST THEN HER BOY-FRIEND WOULD COME ALONG AND POUND ME INTO THE GROUND...

SITTING IN THE DESERT ON A SATURDAY NIGHT TALKING TO A CACTUS ISN'T SO BAD..

I DON'T SUPPOSE YOU'VE DONE MUCH TRAVELING, HAVE YOU?

I'M THINKING OF TAKING A LITTLE TRIP, AND WAS WONDERING IF YOU'D CARE TO GO ALONG...

I'LL ADMIT MY MOTIVE IS A BIT SELFISH..

WITH YOU AROUND, I DON'T THINK I'D EVER GET MUGGED!

NEW YEAR

MISS

OTHMAR

238

PEANUTS

OUR TEACHER, MISS OTHMAR, STAYED HOME TODAY...

YESTERDAY, WE HAD TO BRING MILK MONEY ENVELOPES, CLASS PICTURE MONEY ENVELOPES, PTA MONEY ENVELOPES AND HOT DOG MONEY ENVELOPES...

1-19

THIRTY KIDS BRINGING FOUR ENVELOPES EACH MAKES ONE HUNDRED AND TWENTY ENVELOPES.. POOR MISS OTHMAR...

SHE CRACKED UP... SHE WENT "ENVELOPE HAPPY"!

PEANUTS

DEAR MISS OTHMAR, I HOPE YOU ARE FEELING BETTER.

I DON'T BLAME YOU FOR GETTING UPSET THE OTHER DAY.

1-20

YOU WERE A SIGHT RUNNING DOWN THE HALL SCREAMING AND THROWING THOSE ENVELOPES ALL OVER.

REST QUIETLY. DON'T WORRY ABOUT US.
YOUR PUPIL,
LINUS

SCHULZ

PEANUTS

MISS OTHMAR CAME BACK TO SCHOOL TODAY, BUT SHE DIDN'T LAST VERY LONG..

SEVEN KIDS HAD ABSENCE EXCUSES IN ENVELOPES...

TWENTY-EIGHT OTHERS BROUGHT BACK VACCINATION NOTICES WHICH THEIR PARENTS HAD SIGNED.....
POOR MISS OTHMAR...

1-21

THAT'S THE FIRST TIME I'VE EVER SEEN A TEACHER CRAWL RIGHT UP THE CHALKBOARD!

SCHULZ

PEANUTS

MY TEACHER, MISS OTHMAR, IS GOING TO PUT IN FOR A SALARY CHANGE

A SALARY CHANGE?

YES, SHE SAYS SHE TAKES CHILDREN TO THE MOVIE ROOM FOR MOVIES, TO THE ART ROOM FOR ART, BACK TO THE MOVIE ROOM FOR FILM STRIPS...

3-8

TO THE LIBRARY FOR BOOKS, TO THE CAFETERIA FOR LUNCH, TO THE GYM FOR PHYSICAL EDUCATION AND AROUND AND AROUND THE SCHOOL BUILDING FOR YARD DUTIES...

SHE'S DECIDED SHE WANTS TO BE PAID BY THE MILE!

PEANUTS

MISS OTHMAR?

SLURP SLURP

I WAS WONDERING IF YOU'D CARE TO RECONCILE OUR FAILURE TO SAY "GRACE" BEFORE DRINKING MILK WITH THE STORY OF DANIEL IN THE SIXTH CHAPTER OF THAT BOOK

4-30

OH...

MISS OTHMAR IS NEVER MUCH FOR RECONCILING...

SLURP SLURP

PEANUTS

I DON'T THINK MY TEACHER, MISS OTHMAR, LIKES ME ANY MORE..

SHE DOESN'T LOOK AT ME THE WAY SHE USED TO... SHE DOESN'T EVEN LOOK AT ME AT ALL...

3-25

IT'S A TERRIBLE THING TO DISCOVER THAT YOUR TEACHER DOESN'T LIKE YOU ANY MORE...

IT'S LIKE HAVING A SUBSCRIPTION RUN OUT..

PEANUTS

I'M GOING TO STAND HERE IN THE RAIN UNTIL I CATCH PNEUMONIA, AND DIE...

3-26

IF MISS OTHMAR DOESN'T LIKE ME ANY MORE, I HAVE NOTHING TO LIVE FOR!

I WONDER IF YOU CAN CATCH PNEUMONIA WITHOUT GETTING SO WET?

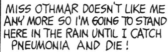

WHERE SHALL WE SIT?

RIGHT OVER THERE

YES, MA'AM? THE BACK ROW? WHY DID I TAKE A SEAT IN THE BACK ROW?

YES, MA'AM, I KNOW THERE ARE SEATS IN THE FRONT ROW... I WAS MERELY OBEYING THE BIBLICAL ADMONITION...

IN THE FOURTEENTH CHAPTER OF LUKE, BEGINNING WITH THE TENTH VERSE, WE READ, "...WHEN YOU ARE INVITED, GO AND SIT IN THE LOWEST PLACE SO THAT WHEN YOUR HOST COMES HE MAY SAY TO YOU, 'FRIEND, GO UP HIGHER';"

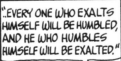

"...EVERY ONE WHO EXALTS HIMSELF WILL BE HUMBLED, AND HE WHO HUMBLES HIMSELF WILL BE EXALTED."

YES, MA'AM..

MISS OTHMAR ISN'T MUCH FOR BIBLICAL ADMONITIONS...

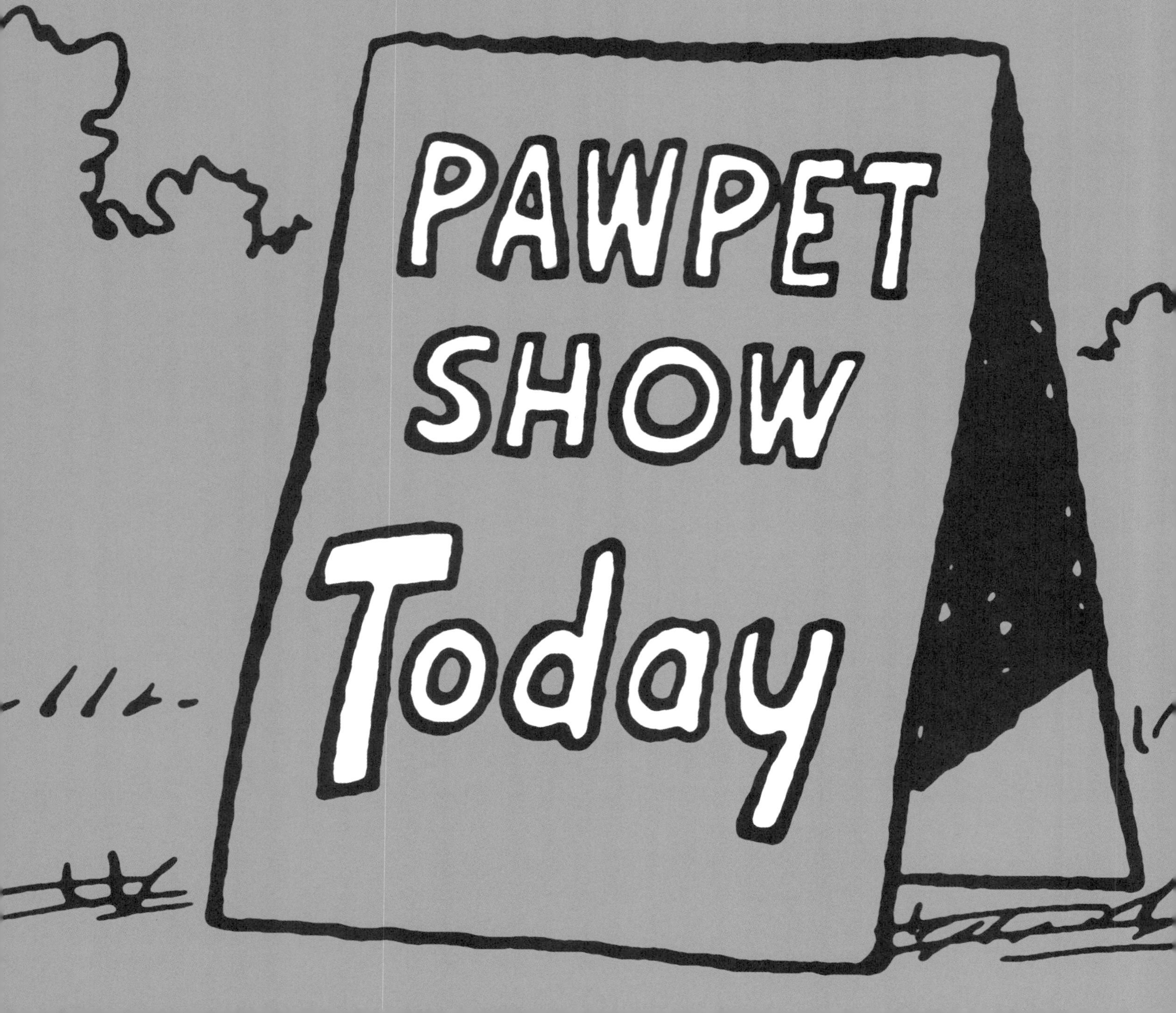
PAWPET
SHOW
Today

PAWPET THEATRE

POW!

POW!

253

· POW!

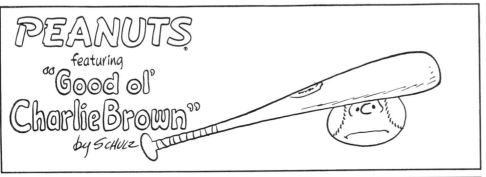

POW!

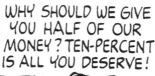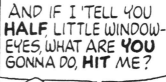

QUEEN SNAKE

PEANUTS

HELP! A QUEEN SNAKE! A QUEEN SNAKE!

1-31

THAT'S NOT A QUEEN SNAKE... THAT'S JUST AN OLD TREE BRANCH

WELL, I'LL BE! SO IT IS!

I SUPPOSE YOU THINK YOU'RE SMART PRETENDING YOU'RE A QUEEN SNAKE!

SCHULZ

PEANUTS

MOM WANTS TO KNOW IF YOU WANT TO GO TO CAMP

CAMP? NOT ON YOUR LIFE!

THOSE CAMPS ARE ALWAYS OUT IN THE WOODS SOME PLACE, AND THOSE WOODS ARE FULL OF QUEEN SNAKES! HAVE YOU EVER BEEN CHOMPED BY A QUEEN SNAKE?

6-13

BOY, YOU GET CHOMPED BY A QUEEN SNAKE, AND YOU'VE HAD IT! YOU WON'T GET ME NEAR ANY WOODS FULL OF QUEEN SNAKES! NO, SIR, NOT ME! I'LL JUST...

I'LL TELL HER YOU'LL BE VERY HAPPY TO GO!

AUGH!

SCHULZ

PEANUTS

SO HERE I AM ON THE BUS HEADED FOR CAMP...

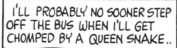

I'LL PROBABLY NO SOONER STEP OFF THE BUS WHEN I'LL GET CHOMPED BY A QUEEN SNAKE...

WHY DO THEY SEND LITTLE KIDS TO CAMP WHO DON'T WANT TO GO?

6-16

I'M DOOMED!

SCHULZ

THE RED BARON

PEANUTS BOY, WHAT A DAY...THIS HAS BEEN THE WORST DAY OF MY LIFE!

I WOKE UP THIS MORNING LOOKING FORWARD TO THE SPELLING BEE, AND I END UP IN THE PRINCIPAL'S OFFICE.... GOOD GRIEF!

ON A DAY LIKE THIS, A PERSON REALLY NEEDS HIS FAITHFUL DOG TO COME RUNNING OUT TO GREET HIM ...

HERE'S THE WORLD WAR I PILOT IN HIS FIGHTER PLANE LOOKING FOR THE RED BARON!

* SIGH *

PEANUTS HERE'S THE WORLD WAR I FLYING ACE POSING BESIDE HIS SOPWITH CAMEL

I AM TAKING OFF FROM AN AERODROME IN FRANCE SOMEWHERE JUST EAST OF PONT-À-MOUSSON...

MY MISSION IS TO SEEK OUT THE RED BARON, AND TO BRING HIM DOWN! **CONTACT!**

SO LONG, CHAPS! WISH ME LUCK!

MY DOG HAS FINALLY FLIPPED!

PEANUTS HERE'S THE WORLD WAR I FLYING ACE ZOOMING THROUGH THE AIR SEARCHING FOR THE 'RED BARON'

AS I PASS OVER METZ, ENEMY BATTERIES BEGIN FIRING...SHELLS BURST BELOW MY SOPWITH CAMEL...

NYAHH, NYAHH, NYAHH!! YOU CAN'T HIT ME!

ACTUALLY, TOUGH FLYING ACES NEVER SAY, 'NYAHH, NYAHH, NYAHH!'

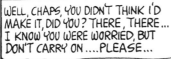

PEANUTS
featuring "Good ol' Charlie Brown"
by Schulz

HERE'S THE WORLD WAR I FLYING ACE BEING AWAKENED TO FLY ANOTHER DAWN PATROL...

HERE'S THE WORLD WAR I FLYING ACE WALKING OUT ONTO THE FIELD...

IT SNOWED LAST NIGHT... BUT TODAY THE SUN IS OUT..THE SKY IS CLEAR..

I CLIMB INTO THE COCKPIT OF MY SOPWITH CAMEL...

"CHOCKS AWAY"

HERE'S THE WORLD WAR I FLYING ACE ZOOMING THROUGH THE AIR SEARCHING FOR THE RED BARON!

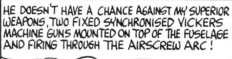

HE DOESN'T HAVE A CHANCE AGAINST MY SUPERIOR WEAPONS, TWO FIXED SYNCHRONISED VICKERS MACHINE GUNS MOUNTED ON TOP OF THE FUSELAGE AND FIRING THROUGH THE AIRSCREW ARC!

POW!

YOU'RE A POOR SPORT, RED BARON

12-11

PEANUTS

DIVING DOWN OUT OF THE CLOUDS I FIRE MY TWIN VICKERS AT THE RED BARON!

HE SWOOPS TO THE LEFT TO AVOID MY FIRE...I SWOOP RIGHT BEHIND HIM...HE SWOOPS TO THE RIGHT...

I SWOOP TO THE RIGHT...HE SWOOPS TO THE LEFT.....I SWOOP TO THE LEFT...HE SWOOPS TO THE RIGHT......I....I...I..

.....I FEEL SICK.....

PEANUTS

HERE'S THE WORLD WAR I FLYING ACE STANDING OUT UNDER THE STARS...IT'S A BEAUTIFUL NIGHT...

SOMEWHERE OFF IN THE DISTANCE IS THE LOW RUMBLE OF ARTILLERY FIRE.. AS HE LOOKS AT THE SKY, HE THINKS OF THE PEOPLE AT HOME, AND WONDERS IF THEY'RE LOOKING AT THE SAME SKY...AND THEN HE IS SAD...

SLOWLY HE WALKS BACK ACROSS THE DARKENED AERODROME, AND THEN THE THOUGHT THAT THROBS SO CONSTANTLY IN HIS MIND CRIES OUT..

CURSE YOU, RED BARON!

PEANUTS

HERE'S THE WORLD WAR I FLYING ACE ZOOMING THROUGH THE AIR SEARCHING FOR THE RED BARON..

MY RIGHT HAND IS ON THE SPADE-GRIP STICK WITH MY THUMB OVER THE GUN TRIGGERS...MY LEFT HAND IS ON THE BENTLEY ROTARY THROTTLE

RATS!

MY RESEARCH IS GOOD, BUT MY FLYING IS LOUSY!

IT'S THE RED BARON! HE'S ON MY TAIL!

1-31

HERE'S WHERE ALL MY MONTHS OF TRAINING WILL COME TO USE...

THE FIRST THING THEY TAUGHT US WAS TO SEEK COVER IN THE CLOUDS

IN TRAINING WE HAD BIGGER CLOUDS

SCHULZ

HERE'S THE WORLD WAR I FLYING ACE BEING CHASED BY THE RED BARON...

2-5

HE HATES ME!

EVERYONE ASKS HOW I KNOW HE HATES ME...

I CAN TELL!

SCHULZ

OH, NO, NOT AGAIN!

I HATE IT WHEN THE RED BARON SHOOTS HOLES IN MY PLANE...

9-3

ALL THE ROOT BEER LEAKS OUT!

SCHULZ

I'VE HEARD THAT OUR CAPTAIN WAS A FIGHTER PILOT DURING THE WAR...

7-29

I DON'T SUPPOSE THOSE EXPERIENCES ARE EASILY FORGOTTEN...

CURSE YOU, RED BARON!

NO, I GUESS NOT

SCHULZ

ROUND-HEADED KID

SECRETARY

SHOW AND TELL

PEANUTS

FOR "SHOW AND TELL" TODAY I HAVE SOMETHING UNIQUE..

4-29

I'M NOT GOING TO TELL ABOUT A PET OR SHOW YOU A TOY OR A BOOK OR SOMETHING LIKE THAT..

INSTEAD, I'M GOING TO TELL YOU ALL ABOUT SOMEONE I CONSIDER QUITE FASCINATING..

MYSELF !!!

SCHULZ

PEANUTS

WELL, HERE I AM AGAIN FOR "SHOW AND TELL"

AND GUESS WHAT I'VE BROUGHT TODAY! I HAVE THINGS IN HERE TO THRILL YOU AND CHILL YOU! I HAVE THINGS IN HERE TO FILL YOU WITH FEAR, WITH TERROR, WITH HORROR! I HAVE THINGS IN HERE TO...

...YES, MA'AM?

ALL THE LIFE HAS GONE OUT OF "SHOW AND TELL"

9-26

SCHULZ

PEANUTS

FOR "SHOW AND TELL" TODAY, I HAVE A LITTLE SURPRISE...

I HAVE BROUGHT THE FIRST SNOWFLAKE OF THE YEAR! NOW, AS YOU MAY OR MAY NOT KNOW, SNOWFLAKES ARE...

11-27

DUE TO CIRCUMSTANCES BEYOND OUR CONTROL, THIS PORTION OF "SHOW AND TELL" HAS BEEN CANCELLED!

SCHULZ

PEANUTS

FOR "SHOW AND TELL" TODAY I HAVE BROUGHT MY PET ROCK..

MY PET ROCK IS AN EXCELLENT GOLFER... HIS FAVORITE COURSE IS "PEBBLE BEACH"!

1-27

HAHAHAHA!

YOU HAVE A PRETTY DULL GROUP HERE, MA'AM

PEANUTS

FOR "SHOW AND TELL" TODAY, I HAVE BROUGHT THIS LEAF

YOU WILL NOTE THAT I LEFT THE TREE WHERE IT WAS!

HA HA HA HA!!!

YES, MA'AM

OKAY, NOW, ABOUT THIS LEAF...

10-24

PEANUTS

TODAY FOR "SHOW AND TELL" I HAVE BROUGHT MY BROTHER'S DOG...

9-13

WHICH MAY TURN OUT TO BE THE BIGGEST MISTAKE OF MY LIFE!

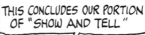

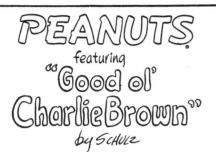

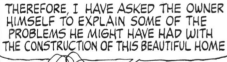

SISTERS

PEANUTS

I STILL DON'T UNDERSTAND HOW YOU COULD THROW YOUR BROTHER OUT OF THE HOUSE WITHOUT FEELING GUILTY..

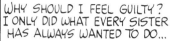

WHY SHOULD I FEEL GUILTY? I ONLY DID WHAT EVERY SISTER HAS ALWAYS WANTED TO DO...

I'LL PROBABLY BE AN INSPIRATION TO EVERY SISTER WHO HAS HAD A BROTHER WHO BUGGED HER! IF I'M AN INSPIRATION, WHY SHOULD I FEEL GUILTY? EVEN YOU SHOULD BE ABLE TO UNDERSTAND THAT, CHARLIE BROWN

I NEVER UNDERSTAND ANYTHING..

PEANUTS

I WAS HERE FIRST SO I GET TO WATCH WHAT I WANT TO WATCH!

HEY!

IN THE NINETEENTH CHAPTER OF THE BOOK OF MATTHEW IT SAYS, "..MANY THAT ARE FIRST WILL BE LAST, AND THE LAST FIRST"

I'LL BET MATTHEW DIDN'T HAVE AN OLDER SISTER!

PEANUTS

BELLE? BELLE?

HOW AM I EVER GOING TO FIND BELLE?

THE LAST I HEARD SHE HAS A TEEN-AGE SON, AND THAT WORTHLESS HOUND SHE MARRIED RAN OFF!

"I GUESS I FORGOT TO TELL YOU THAT BELLE IS MY SISTER...IF IT TURNS OUT THAT SHE NEEDS HELP, WILL YOU SEND SOME MONEY?"

MONEY? I DON'T HAVE ANY MONEY!

HE'S YOUR DOG, CHARLIE BROWN!

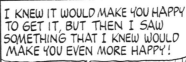

RATS! I TAKE MY STUPID BROTHER SPIKE OUT ON THE TOWN, AND HE RUNS OFF WITH THE FIRST GIRL HE MEETS...

OH, WELL, I'LL GO OVER TO THE CANTEEN AND EAT SOME DOUGHNUTS

MAYBE ONE OF THE RED CROSS GIRLS WILL TALK WITH ME...

BELLE!!! 5-7

BELLE! I DIDN'T KNOW YOU WERE IN THE RED CROSS...WHEN DID YOU GET TO FRANCE?

HOW IS EVERYTHING BACK HOME? DID YOU KNOW I WAS A FLYING ACE? ARE MOM AND DAD PROUD OF ME?

5-8

SPIKE IS HERE, TOO! HE'S IN THE INFANTRY! AND YOU, MY OWN SISTER, IN THE RED CROSS!! I CAN'T BELIEVE IT!

HEY, WHAT HAPPENED TO ALL THE DOUGHNUTS?

YOU ATE THEM!

HEY, SPIKE! WHERE HAVE YOU BEEN? LOOK WHO'S HERE..OUR SISTER BELLE... SHE'S IN THE RED CROSS!

WE'RE ALL TOGETHER! I CAN'T BELIEVE IT!

THIS CALLS FOR A CELEBRATION...

5-9

ROOT BEER ALL AROUND!

I KNOW WHAT WE SHOULD DO! WE'RE ALL TOGETHER HERE SO WE SHOULD HAVE OUR PICTURE TAKEN...

WE'LL SEND IT HOME TO MOM AND DAD...

And that's the story of how two soldiers and their sister met in France during World War I.

5-11

And I don't care if anyone believes me or not.

SNOWMAN

PEANUTS

BOY, WHAT A DIRTY DEAL! THAT STUPID REFEREE!

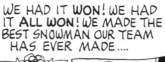

WE HAD IT **WON**! WE HAD IT **ALL WON**! WE MADE THE BEST SNOWMAN OUR TEAM HAS EVER MADE....

THEN YOU KNOW WHAT HAPPENED? THAT STUPID REFEREE PENALIZED US FOR "IMPROPER MITTENS"!

"IMPROPER MITTENS"?

PEANUTS

WHAT ARE YOU DOING?

I'M FILLING OUT AN INSURANCE FORM...

ALL "SNOW LEAGUERS" HAVE TO TO BE COVERED IN CASE WE'RE INJURED WHILE BUILDING A SNOWMAN

I SUPPOSE IF A SNOWMAN FELL ON YOU, IT COULD BE QUITE SERIOUS

THAT'S WHY WE HAVE TEN THOUSAND DOLLARS COVERAGE...

IT'S DEFINITELY A HIGH-RISK SPORT!

PEANUTS

MY TEAM IS WINNING, BIG BROTHER! WE'RE WINNING!

SEE? WE'RE BUILDING A BETTER SNOWMAN THAN THEY ARE! WE'RE WINNING!

WHAT'S THAT?!

OFFSIDE?!! HOW CAN A SNOWMAN BE OFFSIDE?! YOU STUPID REFEREE!!!

PEANUTS WE'LL DEFY THEM ALL, SNOOPY!

WE WILL? WE'LL BUILD OUR OWN SNOWMAN WITHOUT BELONGING TO ANY TEAM OR ORGANIZATION!

12-7

IF THEY FIND OUT, WE'LL DEFY THEM! WE'LL STAND UP FOR OUR RIGHTS!

I'M TOO YOUNG TO BE A TEST CASE!

SCHULZ

PEANUTS WHAT WOULD HAPPEN IF I SNEAKED OUT INTO MY BACK YARD AND MADE A SNOWMAN WITHOUT ADULT SUPERVISION?

12-6

I'LL DO IT!

SCHULZ

PSST, SNOOPY! WANNA HELP ME MAKE A SNOWMAN? AT TWO O'CLOCK IN THE MORNING?

CALL ME WHEN THE SNOW IS WARMER!

SCHULZ

PEANUTS HA! I GUESS I SHOWED YOU GUYS!

12-8

I BUILT MY OWN SNOWMAN IN MY OWN BACK YARD, AND I DID IT WITHOUT BELONGING TO A TEAM OR A LEAGUE OR ANYTHING!

WHO CARES? WE'RE INTO BOWLING NOW! WE HAVE SPONSORS AND TROPHIES AND DINNERS AND EVERYTHING!

I HOPE YOU MISS THE FIVE PIN!! AND MAY ALL YOUR SPLITS BE SEVEN-TEN!

SCHULZ

SUPPERTIME!

PEANUTS

MY STOMACH TELLS ME IT'S SUPPERTIME

RATS!

3-27

IT ISN'T EVEN **NEAR** SUPPERTIME...

I HATE HAVING A STOMACH THAT TELLS LIES!

SCHULZ

PEANUTS

SUPPERTIME!

2-21

HOW GAUCHE, BUT NICE

HEAD BEAGLE

SCHULZ

PEANUTS

SUPPERTIME!

3-23

GOOD GRIEF! WHAT HAPPENED TO YOUR DOG HOUSE?

NEVER MIND!

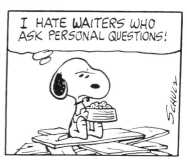

I HATE WAITERS WHO ASK PERSONAL QUESTIONS!

SCHULZ

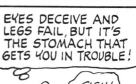

HOW DO DOGS ALWAYS SEEM TO KNOW WHEN IT'S TIME TO EAT?

THEY DON'T HAVE CLOCKS OR WATCHES..

HOW DO YOU ALWAYS KNOW THAT IT'S SUPPERTIME?

I STAY IN CLOSE COMMUNICATION WITH MY STOMACH

12-29

SUPPERTIME ISN'T FOR ANOTHER HOUR...

AND STOP STARING AT THE BACK DOOR..IT MAKES ME NERVOUS!

THAT'S THE IDEA

4-6

SUPPERTIME!

7-29

JUST IN CASE YOU'RE INTERESTED..

THIS MEAL WAS PROVIDED BY FUNDS FROM THE PRIVATE SECTOR

MY COMPLIMENTS TO THE PRIVATE SECTOR!

SUPPERTIME!

LOOKS PRETTY GOOD, DOESN'T IT?

ACTUALLY, IT LOOKED BETTER FROM A DISTANCE!

9-12

TENNIS

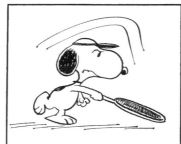

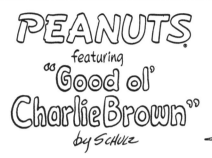

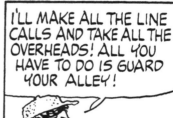

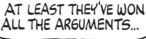

I WOULD LIKE TO THANK EVERYONE FOR THIS FINE TOURNAMENT WE HAD HERE TODAY..THE FANS.. THE LINE JUDGES...

AND, OF COURSE, THE BALL BIRDS!

THANKS-
GIVING

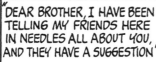

HERE YOU ARE, SPIKE...

HERE'S YOUR THANKSGIVING DINNER...TURKEY, MASHED POTATOES, GRAVY AND CRANBERRY SAUCE!

I CAN'T HELP BUT WONDER WHAT KIND OF DINNER SNOOPY IS HAVING OUT THERE ON THE DESERT WITH THE COYOTES...

THESE PEOPLE EAT **BUNNIES**!!

WHAT A LOUSY THANKSGIVING!

THOSE STUPID COYOTES ARE COMPLETELY UNCIVILIZED... THEY EAT BUNNIES!

I'M GOING HOME WHERE I CAN HAVE A GOOD OLD-FASHIONED CAN OF REAL DOG FOOD!

BUNNIES! I CAN'T BELIEVE IT...HOW GROSS!

WELL, SO LONG, SPIKE

I'M GLAD YOU COULD SPEND THANKSGIVING WITH US

KEEP AN EYE OUT FOR SNOOPY... I HAVE A FEELING YOU MIGHT MEET HIM ON THE WAY...

ALL BEAGLES LOOK ALIKE TO ME!

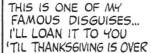

TYPEWRITER

PEANUTS | As he touched her hand, she sighed...

STOP RAINING ON MY NOVEL!

PEANUTS | And they lived happily ever after.

The End

FOR THE FIRST TIME IN MY LIFE, I KNOW HOW LEO MUST HAVE FELT...

LEO TOLSTOY, THAT IS!

PEANUTS | I was born one bright Spring morning at the Daisy Hill Puppy Farm.

I was one of seven puppies. My father and mother loved me.

Those were happy days.

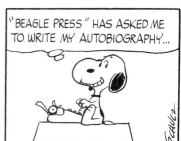

"BEAGLE PRESS" HAS ASKED ME TO WRITE MY AUTOBIOGRAPHY...

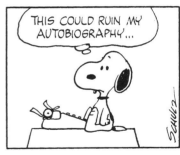

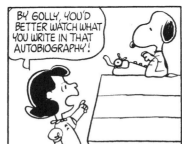

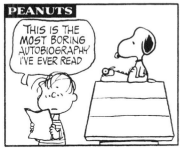

Everything

Everything You Always

Everything You Always Wanted To Know About Beagles, But Were Afraid To Ask

PEANUTS

those years in Paris were to be among the finest of her life.

Looking back, she once remarked, "Those years in Paris were among the finest of my life." That was what she said when she looked back upon those years in Paris

where she spent some of the finest years of her life.

I THINK THIS IS GOING TO NEED A LITTLE EDITING...

PEANUTS

Now is the time for all foxes to jump over the lazy dog.

SOMEHOW, THAT DOESN'T SEEM QUITE RIGHT...

PEANUTS

Things I've Learned
After It Was Too Late

6-28

Never argue with the cat
next door. He's always right

SCHULZ

PEANUTS

Things I've Learned After
It was Too late.

A whole stack of
memories will never
equal one little hope.

7-1

I KIND OF
LIKE THAT

SCHULZ

PEANUTS

9-25

To Whom It May
Concern;

Dear Whom,

SCHULZ

PEANUTS

The Bunnies - A Tale of
Mirth and Woe.

"Ha Ha Ha," laughed
the bunnies.

"Ha Ha Ha Ha Ha Ha
Ha Ha Ha Ha Ha Ha"

SO MUCH FOR
THE MIRTH!

4-25

SCHULZ

PEANUTS

Gentlemen,

8-31

Well, another day has gone by and you still haven't come to pick up my novel for publication.

Just for that, I am going to offer it to another publisher.

Nyahh! Nyahh! Nyahh!

PEANUTS

Gentlemen, I have just completed my new novel.

8-29

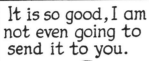

It is so good, I am not even going to send it to you.

Why don't you just come and get it?

PEANUTS

Gentlemen,

8-30

Yesterday, I waited all day for you to come and get my novel and to publish it and make me rich and famous.

You did not show up.

Were you not feeling well?

PEANUTS

"Do you love me?" she asked.
"Of course," he said.

10-15

"Do you really love me?" she asked.
"Of course," he said.

"Do you really really love me?" she asked.
"No," he said.

"Do you love me?" she asked.
"Of course," he said.
So she asked no more.

PEANUTS

"Our love will last forever," he said.

10-17

"Oh, yes, yes, yes!" she cried.

"Forever being a relative term, however," he said.

She hit him with a ski pole.

PEANUTS

DEAR SIR...

8-28

Dˣy²RkiQL&
!c"h m s
? 3 d? ---
f B
*

MY SECRETARY ISN'T USED TO AN ELECTRIC TYPEWRITER!

UNREQUITED LOVE

PEANUTS

I THINK I'LL GO OVER AND INTRODUCE MYSELF TO THAT LITTLE RED-HAIRED GIRL

I THINK I'LL INTRODUCE MYSELF, AND THEN ASK HER TO COME OVER AND SIT NEXT TO ME

I THINK I'LL ASK HER TO SIT NEXT TO ME HERE, AND THEN I THINK I'LL TELL HER HOW MUCH I'VE ALWAYS ADMIRED HER...

10-21

I THINK I'LL FLAP MY ARMS, AND FLY TO THE MOON

PEANUTS

IT'S STUPID TO JUST SIT HERE AND ADMIRE THAT LITTLE RED-HAIRED GIRL FROM A DISTANCE

3-23

IT'S STUPID NOT TO GET UP AND GO OVER AND TALK TO HER...IT'S REALLY STUPID...IT'S JUST PLAIN STUPID...

SO WHY DON'T I GO OVER AND TALK TO HER?

BECAUSE I'M STUPID!

PEANUTS

I'D GIVE ANYTHING TO BE ABLE TO TALK WITH THAT LITTLE RED-HAIRED GIRL...

3-24

THE AMAZING THING IS THAT I **KNOW** I'M THE SORT OF PERSON SHE'D LIKE! I MEAN I'M NOT ROUGH OR CRUDE OR ANYTHING

I'M NOT THE GREATEST PERSON WHO EVER LIVED, OF COURSE, BUT AFTER ALL, WHO IS? I'M JUST A NICE SORT OF GUY WHO....

..WHO NEVER GETS TO MEET LITTLE RED-HAIRED GIRLS!

PEANUTS WHAT'S THIS? THAT LITTLE RED-HAIRED GIRL DROPPED HER PENCIL...

GEE...IT'S GOT TEETH MARKS ALL OVER IT...

SHE NIBBLES ON HER PENCIL...

SHE'S HUMAN!

3-25

PEANUTS WHAT'S THAT YOU'RE HOLDING?

IT'S A PENCIL...IT BELONGS TO THAT LITTLE RED-HAIRED GIRL... I'M GOING TO STAND HERE UNTIL SHE WALKS BY, AND THEN I'M GOING TO TELL HER HOW I FOUND IT...

3-26

I HATE TO SEE YOU GO TO ALL THAT TROUBLE, CHARLIE BROWN... WHY DON'T I JUST GIVE IT TO HER?

HEY! HERE'S YOUR STUPID PENCIL!!

PEANUTS DID YOU SEE THE BULLETIN BOARD? GOOD LUCK, CHARLIE BROWN!

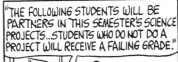

"THE FOLLOWING STUDENTS WILL BE PARTNERS IN THIS SEMESTER'S SCIENCE PROJECTS...STUDENTS WHO DO NOT DO A PROJECT WILL RECEIVE A FAILING GRADE."

GOOD GRIEF! I'VE BEEN PAIRED WITH THAT PRETTY, LITTLE RED-HAIRED GIRL! HOW CAN I BE HER PARTNER? I CAN'T EVEN **TALK** TO HER!

SUDDENLY I HAVE THE FEELING OF IMPENDING DOOM!

11-7

PEANUTS OH, OH! THAT LITTLE RED-HAIRED GIRL IS LOOKING AT THE BULLETIN BOARD..

NOW SHE KNOWS THAT THE TEACHER HAS MADE US PARTNERS IN THE SCIENCE PROJECT! MAYBE SHE'LL COME OVER HERE AND SAY, "HI, CHARLIE BROWN..I SEE YOU AND I ARE PARTNERS!"

11-8

MAYBE SHE'LL EVEN OFFER TO SHAKE HANDS...I'LL BET HER HANDS ARE SMOOTH AND COOL...

MY HEAD IS HOT AND STUPID!

PEANUTS

THAT LITTLE RED-HAIRED GIRL HAS COME TO WATCH OUR GAME..

8-12

I WONDER IF SHE'S LOOKING AT ME.......

SHE WASN'T LOOKING AT ME...

PEANUTS

WHAT ARE YOU DOING, CHARLIE BROWN? WHY DON'T YOU PITCH?

THAT LITTLE RED-HAIRED GIRL..SHE'S WATCHING THE GAME...

OH, GOOD GRIEF!

THIS IS MY BIG CHANCE TO BE A HERO, AND SHE'S WATCHING!

I'M GOING TO BEAR DOWN AND PITCH A GREAT GAME, AND THAT LITTLE RED-HAIRED GIRL WILL BE SO IMPRESSED AND SO EXCITED THAT SHE'LL RUSH OUT HERE TO THE MOUND AND GIVE ME A BIG HUG, AND.....

8-13

OH, BROTHER! WHY DO I THINK ABOUT THINGS LIKE THAT?

PEANUTS

GOOD GRIEF, CHARLIE BROWN, WHEN ARE YOU GOING TO THROW THE FIRST PITCH?

THAT LITTLE RED-HAIRED GIRL IS WATCHING...I CAN'T LET GO OF THE BALL..MY FINGERS ARE NUMB

8-14

I'M STARTING TO SHAKE..LOOK AT ME! I'M SHAKING ALL OVER!

I DON'T SUPPOSE THERE'S A NEUROLOGIST IN THE STANDS..

WOULDN'T A GENERAL PRACTITIONER DO?

HOW ABOUT A VET?

PEANUTS

COME ON, CHARLIE BROWN..WE'LL TAKE YOU HOME..

I'M GOING TO PITCH A GREAT GAME..

8-15

THAT LITTLE RED-HAIRED GIRL IS WATCHING, AND I'M GOING TO PITCH A GREAT GAME, AND SHE'S GOING TO BE IMPRESSED, AND...

WE'LL TAKE YOU HOME, CHARLIE BROWN, AND YOU CAN GO TO BED UNTIL YOU STOP SHAKING...

I'M GOING TO BE THE HERO AND PITCH A GREAT GAME AND THAT LITTLE RED-HAIRED GIRL WILL BE WATCHING AND I'LL BE PITCHING AND I'LL BE GREAT AND SHE'LL BE THERE AN..

PEANUTS

OKAY, START THE GAME!

I FEEL BETTER! I'VE STOPPED SHAKING!

THE GAME'S OVER, CHARLIE BROWN, AND GUESS WHAT... **WE WON!**

LINUS TOOK YOUR PLACE... HE PITCHED A GREAT GAME... AND THERE WAS THIS LITTLE RED-HAIRED GIRL WATCHING...

8-16

SHE GOT SO EXCITED AFTER THE GAME THAT SHE RUSHED OUT TO THE MOUND, AND GAVE LINUS A BIG HUG!

AAUGH!

PEANUTS

MY FRIEND

MY FRIEND, THE RELIEF PITCHER

MY FRIEND, THE RELIEF PITCHER, WHO PITCHED A GREAT GAME, AND IMPRESSED THAT LITTLE RED-HAIRED GIRL SO MUCH THAT SHE RAN OUT AND GAVE HIM A BIG HUG!

17

MY FRIEND!

PEANUTS

I'LL NEVER GET TO MEET THAT LITTLE RED-HAIRED GIRL...

SOMETIMES I GET SO DEPRESSED I CAN HARDLY STAND IT..

ONE BOWL, PLEASE..

GOOP 5¢

A GOOD WAY TO FORGET A LOVE AFFAIR IS TO EAT A LOT OF GOOP!

6-1

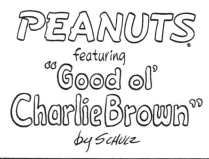

VALENTINES

370

PEANUTS

I GOT A VALENTINE FROM JOYCE!

2-15

AND I GOT ONE FROM SHIRLEY, AND FROM BARBARA, AND FROM SUE, AND FROM VIRGINIA, AND FROM PAT, AND FROM KAY, AND..

I HATE SOMEONE WHO GLOATS OVER ALL HIS VALENTINES!

THE FIFTEENTH OF FEBRUARY IS ALWAYS "GLOAT DAY"!

PEANUTS

AND I GOT A VALENTINE FROM DONNA, AND FROM AMY, AND FROM JILL...

AND I GOT ONE FROM CHARLENE, AND FROM MARTHA, AND FROM ...

IT'S VERY GAUCHE TO BRAG ABOUT ALL YOUR VALENTINES!

2-16

IT IS?

OH, WELL! AND I GOT ONE FROM JOAN, AND FROM QUINTANA, AND FROM MEREDITH, AND FROM...

SIGH

PEANUTS

SOMETIMES A VALENTINE WILL GET LOST IN THE MAIL

3-6

SOMETIMES A VALENTINE WILL GET LOST IN THE MAIL, AND NOT ARRIVE UNTIL WEEKS LATER..

SOMETIMES

WORLD FAMOUS

PEANUTS

HERE'S THE WORLD-FAMOUS NOVELIST WALKING TO THE MAILBOX TO SEND HIS LATEST MANUSCRIPT AWAY..

U.S. MAIL

HERE, LET ME HELP YOU...

MY CAREER ALMOST CAME TO AN END!

U.S. MAIL

PEANUTS

HERE'S THE WORLD-FAMOUS ASTRONAUT APPROACHING THE MOON..

FANTASTIC!

IT LOOKS LIKE A DIRTY BEACH...

OR HAS SOMEONE ALREADY SAID THAT?

PEANUTS

HERE'S THE WORLD FAMOUS HOCKEY PLAYER SITTING IN THE PENALTY BOX..

I HATE EVERYBODY!

I'M MEAN! I'M TOUGH!

I EAT GOALIES!

PEANUTS

HERE'S THE WORLD FAMOUS FOOTBALL COACH WALKING OUT ONTO THE FIELD

WINNING IS EVERYTHING! LOSING IS LIKE NOTHING!

THIS YEAR WE'RE GOING TO STRESS PHYSICAL CONDITIONING.. LOTS OF PUSH-UPS AND PLENTY OF RUNNING...

9-2

?

WOODSTOCK ALWAYS HAS TROUBLE WITH PUSH-UPS

PEANUTS

BUTTER.. NINETY-EIGHT TWICE.. BREAD.. THIRTY-NINE..

8-25

HERE'S THE WORLD FAMOUS GROCERY CLERK WORKING AT THE CHECK-OUT COUNTER...

EGGS...FIFTY-NINE..TEA... SEVENTY-NINE... MILK...

ACTUALLY, THERE AREN'T MORE THAN A DOZEN WORLD-FAMOUS GROCERY CLERKS...

PEANUTS

LOOK, CHARLIE BROWN...IT'S AN ANNOUNCEMENT ABOUT A SCHOOL SKI TRIP...

SKI

THEY TAKE US ON A BUS TO "LOFTY MOUNTAIN," AND WE STAY AT A LODGE AND THEY TEACH US TO SKI AND EVERYTHING...

12-15

SHALL WE SIGN UP?

I WONDER WHO ELSE IS GOING?

HERE'S THE WORLD-FAMOUS SKIER HEADING FOR THE SLOPES...

PEANUTS

HOW ARE YOUR KNEES TODAY?

THEY FEEL BETTER..AT LEAST I CAN WALK WITHOUT IT KILLING ME

ARE YOU GOING SKATING AGAIN?

7-4

NO, I GAVE MY SKATES AWAY TO SOMEONE WHO REALLY THINKS HE CAN USE THEM...

HERE'S THE WORLD-FAMOUS ROLLER DERBY STAR GOING INTO THE FAR TURN!

HERE'S THE WORLD FAMOUS BEAGLE SCOUT STARTING OFF ON A ROCK HUNTING EXPEDITION..

AH! HERE'S A NICE ONE...

OOOO! HERE'S A BEAUTY!

AH!

THIS IS YOUR ROCK COLLECTION? LET ME SEE...

BOY, WHAT A DUMB LOOKING ROCK COLLECTION! IT LOOKS LIKE YOU FOUND THEM ALL IN A DRIVEWAY!

NO ONE WOULD EVER BE INTERESTED IN A BUNCH OF ROCKS LIKE THAT..

NOT EVEN THEIR MOTHERS?

YES

MA'AM

YES MA'AM

382

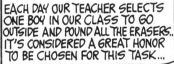

PEANUTS

YES, MA'AM? MY NAME?

MY NAME IS SALLY BROWN, AND I HATE SCHOOL!

PLEASE, DON'T CRY...

PEANUTS

THE PRINCIPAL'S OFFICE? YES, MA'AM..

NOW, WHAT IN THE WORLD DOES THE PRINCIPAL WANT TO SEE **ME** ABOUT? MAYBE HE WANTS ME TO MANAGE THE SCHOOL BALL TEAM THIS NEXT SEASON...I DOUBT IT..

GOING TO THE PRINCIPAL'S OFFICE IS A SCARY THING...

I THINK THEY PURPOSELY PUT THE DOOR KNOB UP HIGH TO MAKE YOU FEEL INFERIOR!

PEANUTS

MY SCIENCE PROJECT? YES, MA'AM..I HAVE IT READY TO SHOW TO THE CLASS..

AT FIRST I HAD A LITTLE TROUBLE TRYING TO DECIDE WHAT TO DO, BUT HERE IT IS......

TOAST!!

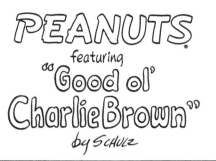

PEANUTS featuring "Good ol' Charlie Brown" by Schulz

YES, MA'AM..

MY REPORT IS ON POPULATION CONTROL...

PEOPLE ARE EVERYWHERE.. SOME PEOPLE SAY THERE ARE TOO MANY OF US, BUT NO ONE WANTS TO LEAVE..

WHAT'S SO FUNNY ?!

BY GOLLY, THIS IS A SERIOUS REPORT! YOU'D BETTER STOP LAUGHING!

I DON'T HAVE TO STAND FOR THIS!

I CAN WALK OUT OF THIS SCHOOL, YOU KNOW! I CAN GO TO MY LOCKER AND GET MY COAT AND MY BOOKS AND LEAVE !!

AND THAT'S JUST WHAT I'M GONNA DO! GOOD-BY !!

1-24

YES, MA'AM ?

I FORGOT MY LOCKER COMBINATION..

PEANUTS

YES, MA'AM...THAT'S MY BOOK REPORT..

WHAT ARE THE ODDS ON A LITTLE LOVE AND UNDERSTANDING?

PEANUTS

NO, MA'AM, I DIDN'T WEAR A DRESS TODAY BECAUSE I'VE DECIDED TO DEFY THE DRESS CODE

I DON'T THINK IT'S FAIR...YES, MA'AM... I UNDERSTAND...

SO LONG, FRANKLIN.. THIS IS IT!

WRITE TO ME IN CARE OF THE TOWER OF LONDON!

PEANUTS

COULD YOU REPEAT THE QUESTION, MA'AM?

YES, MA'AM... I UNDERSTAND..

"WHAT WAS THE AUTHOR'S PURPOSE IN WRITING THIS STORY?"

MAYBE HE NEEDED THE MONEY!

YES, MA'AM, I'M ALL READY FOR THE TEST

I HAVE THREE SHARP PENCILS...

FIVE SHEETS OF CLEAN PAPER...

AND LOTS OF ERASERS!

SUBTRACTION?

OH, YES, MA'AM

11-13

I CAN EXPLAIN IT

SUBTRACTION IS THE AWFUL FEELING THAT YOU KNOW LESS TODAY THAN YOU DID YESTERDAY

WHO, ME?

9-21

YES, MA'AM, I THINK MY REPORT IS READY...

ANYWAY, I'LL GIVE IT MY BEST SHOT

JUST A LITTLE COLLOQUIALISM, THERE, MA'AM

I'VE GOT IT!

YES, MA'AM, I THINK I KNOW THE ANSWER

SIXTEEN.. FOUR.. THIRTY-SEVEN

9-12

ON SECOND THOUGHT, THAT MAY BE MY LOCKER COMBINATION!

AHEM

THIS IS MY REPORT ON...

12-13

MA'AM? YES, MA'AM..

THIS IS REALLY ME!

YES, MA'AM, THE SNOW IS COMING THROUGH THE CEILING AGAIN...

1-25

RIGHT UP THERE, SEE? RIGHT THROUGH THAT HOLE THERE IN THE CEILING...

NO, IT'S NOT FALLING ON MOST OF US

JUST US D MINUS TYPES!

YES, MA'AM, MY ATTORNEY AND I WOULD LIKE TO SEE THE PRINCIPAL..WE'RE GOING TO SUE HIM!

BECAUSE I'M ALL WET, THAT'S WHY! THE CEILING IN OUR ROOM LEAKS, AND IT RAINS ON MY HEAD!

MY ATTORNEY HAS GIVEN THIS CASE A LOT OF THOUGHT...

1-30

"WHEN YOU GO INTO AN ATTORNEY'S OFFICE DOOR, YOU WILL HAVE TO PAY FOR IT FIRST OR LAST"

A LOT OF THOUGHT

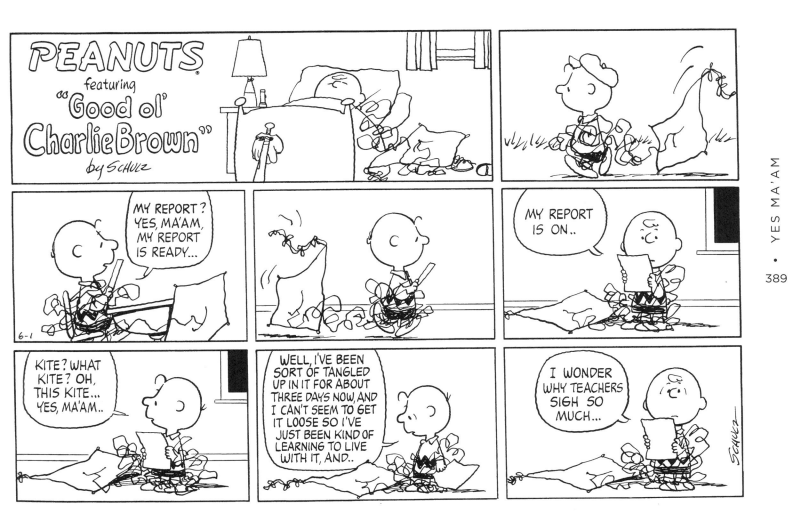

N

Z

392

PEANUTS

DO YOU WANT TO HEAR MY REPORT ON ABRAHAM LINCOLN?

"TODAY IS ABRAHAM LINCOLN'S BIRTHDAY...WHO, YOU MAY ASK, WAS ABRAHAM LINCOLN? OKAY, I'LL TELL YOU...ABRAHAM LINCOLN WAS OUR SIXTEENTH KING AND HE WAS THE FATHER OF LOT'S WIFE..."

2-12

DO YOU THINK I SHOULD MENTION ABOUT HIS PICTURE BEING ON ALL THOSE PENNIES?

THAT MIGHT BE INTERESTING

DO YOU THINK I'LL GET AN "A"?

DO THEY GIVE OUT "Z'S"?

SCHULZ

PEANUTS

WE GOT OUR TESTS BACK...

I WONDER WHAT GRADE I GOT...I HATE TO LOOK...

11-14

"Z MINUS"?!!

SCHULZ

PEANUTS

PRINCIPAL'S OFFICE

YES, SIR...I'D LIKE TO PROTEST A GRADE THAT MY TEACHER GAVE ME ON OUR LAST TEST...

LOOK...A "Z MINUS"!

11-15

THAT'S NOT A GRADE... THAT'S SARCASM!!

SCHULZ

GET THE WHOLE GANG!
Complete your collection

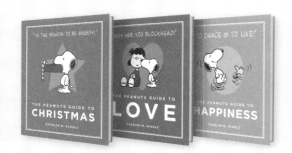
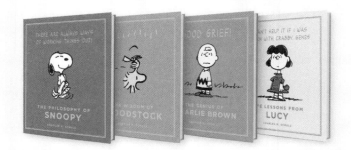